The *Lord's*

P

C000094019

the 7 Chakras,

the 12 Life Paths

**the prayer of Christ Consciousness
as a light for the auric centers
and a map through the
archetypal paths
of astrology**

Dana Williams

Attunement Press

Paperback Version:

ISBN-13: 978-0-9795995-7-6
ISBN-10: 0-9795995-7-1

Dedicated in gratitude to Joe Koperski,
who taught white light meditation to me
when I was still very young

Contents

Introduction

As a young and ardent student of meditation, it came to me that the phrases of the Lord's Prayer—the very heart of the Christian faith—correspond perfectly to the esoteric qualities of the chakras. Speaking the prayer in my mind, I mentally traveled through the chakras, from the seventh chakra downwards. The effect was immediate and profound. Tears streamed down my cheeks. I was lifted into a feeling of peace and renewal. I had a sense of coming home.

At this time, I also studied astrology. I was fascinated by this ancient language of symbols (based on four elements, four seasons, and the wheel) that aimed to describe the complexity of human nature, the unfolding of human life, and the relationship between small, finite human lives and the seemingly infinite universe. One day, I again had a sudden insight: I perceived that the individual phrases of the Lord's Prayer also fit perfectly into the twelve archetypal paths of life as symbolized by the twelve divisions of the Zodiac wheel. Saying the prayer and holding the twelve paths in mind, I again felt a deep inner alignment.

If we start a spiritual practice and keep it up over many years, even if we periodically neglect to do it, the practice will grow, change and deepen. After 35 years of the Lord's Prayer Chakra and Life Paths meditations, I feel honored to write this book, a simple treatment of sorts, to introduce the reader to the practice as well.

Once the initial learning curve has been taken, reciting the Lord's Prayer in the chakras and/or the 12 life paths is easy to do. It requires little time, can be done both sitting up in prayer or meditation, or lying down before sleep or before rising in the morning. The Lord's Prayer Chakra and 12 Path Meditation is always powerful and rejuvenating. Spanning the arc between western and eastern spiritual traditions, the lessons it teaches and the insights it provides are never-ending.

For whom is this book written? For those interested in the correlations and prayer-meditations described here, for those who treasure the Christian traditions and the esoteric sciences, and for those who work sincerely with prayer. If enacted with sincerity and focus, this prayer-meditation has an immediate, uplifting and renewing effect. The purpose of this book is to open the door to this experience.

Dana Williams, May 2009

Thanks and Acknowledgement

When I was eleven years old, Pastor Schaller introduced me to Christianity. His sermons described the beauty and joy of a trusting, intimate relationship with God—one that, he said, is every human being's natural born right. I was a sincere Bible-reading Christian Fundamentalist until nearly fifteen, when I became interested in world religions, broader spiritual experience, and universal spiritual language. I am grateful to have been a fundamentalist for a little while, as it opened my mind and heart to direct inner communion with spirit and with the Christ consciousness archetype.

When I was seventeen, I was privileged to join a small circle of students taught by Joseph Koperski. Joe's white-light, chakra-charging and aura-expanding meditation integrated prayers and passages from the Bible. I studied with Joe for two years, three evenings a week, three hours each evening. It was while studying with Joe that I developed the Lord's Prayer Meditation through the chakras and the twelve life paths.

At the age of twenty-five, I joined the circle of students attending Hugo Maier, also known as Appa, whose ashram today continues in India. Appa was a master in the tradition of Ramana Maharishi, Ramdas, and Anandamayi Ma, three celebrated spiritual teachers from Tamil Southern India. Appa taught a form of meditation based on direct inner experience, and, at times, went deeply into the chakras. He often discussed the history and truths of all religions, including Christianity. For two months each summer, and for seven consecutive years, I sat with him and his students for five to eight hours a day.

I practiced on my own during my thirties and forties while raising my family. Life with children was often very busy, and I found it difficult to find time and concentration for a spiritual practice such as yoga or deep meditation. But the Lord's Prayer Meditation was always possible: a few minutes before getting out of bed in the morning or before going to sleep at night was all the time needed.

This practice remained a source of sustenance through many wonderful but difficult years. During this time, I was diagnosed with a degenerative disease. On many mornings, when I lay paralyzed by fatigue in bed, I was able to renew my energy, activate my nerves, get out of bed and function relatively well after this prayer-meditation. I was eventually able to heal using alternative medicine and dietary therapies. I am certain that my healing was greatly supported by the Lord's Prayer Meditation that I have kept up all these years.

Thank you to the teachers!

Part One

The Lord's Prayer
and the Chakras

1. The Chakras

Chakras can be conceived as energy centers or stations in the human energy field, or as subtle energy organs that metabolize energy (receive, assimilate and express), and that maintain the health of the body, mind, and spirit. Each chakra corresponds to a major nerve bundle or ganglia in the body, to an endocrinal gland, to a state of consciousness, and to an aspect of personality and life. They all feed into a core energy column that extends from the top of the head to the base of the spine. This column is linked through an energy vortex-funnel to the blissful energy of pure consciousness above the head, and to vitalizing primal earth energy downward from the base of the spine. Thus, each person's energy body, also called the aura, is a bridge between the spiritual and earth forces, and represents our dual nature: earth being, spirit being.

I have found that the Lord's Prayer works as a "user's manual" for the human chakra system. Each of its phrases suggests a specific attitude conducive to spiritual growth, and that fits into a chakra like a key into a lock. By reciting each phrase within its appropriate chakra, we create an impulse or evocation that brings us into harmony with Spirit's intention for our growth.

The Lord's Prayer prayer-meditation begins at the highest chakra of pure consciousness at the top of the head. We thus first connect with pure spirit and then bring this impulse down into the lower chakras as we continue with the prayer. This brings the impulse of highest spirituality into all the chakras and—day by day, year for year—transforms the patterns of ego that block the impulse of Spirit in our life.

Colors of the Chakras

Some people called clairvoyants can see the energy body and the chakras. They report that if the auric colors are clear and radiant, good health and a positive attitude can be expected. If the colors are dark or muddy, toxic health or toxic thoughts can be expected. In a successful healing process of both the body and the mind, muddy colors are transformed into radiant colors.

Even if the colors or emotions in one's aura are dark and muddy, however, and we feel weak, ill, angry or oppressed, if we can just sit quietly and let our energies/emotions *be*, (non-judgmentally, without the mind exerting criticism), one's energy system will automatically balance itself again, leaving us feeling uplifted, relieved, and positive. This self-healing process will be referred to in this book as *direct inner experience meditation*.

2. Essential Elements

From Above to Below

The Chakra Meditation described in this book begins at the top of the head and works its way down to the feet. This direction is unusual in chakra work, which usually starts at the base of the spine and moves upwards. In her book, "Sacred Contracts," the intuitive healer Caroline Myss discusses a similar approach. She suggests discovering our personal archetypes in the energetic sphere above the head (the eighth chakra). She describes bringing these archetypes down through the chakras as a form of inner work. The purpose is to understand how our archetypes (deeply held beliefs, behaviors and drives) affect us in each area of our life (chakras), and to bring transformation to these areas. According to this view, the Lord's Prayer Chakra Meditation that I describe here would bring the Christ Consciousness archetype down through the chakras and thus give each area of life a spiritual impulse from that higher consciousness. Another remarkable teacher who taught chakra meditation in the direction of the higher to the lower was Rudolf Steiner, the founder of Anthroposophy. Steiner described his chakra meditation as personal transformation through Christ Consciousness.

Direct Inner Experience Meditation

The Lord's Prayer Meditation does not require that we practice direct inner experience meditation, but if you have time and interest, you might look into it. Direct inner experience meditation allow us to discover an absolute home base to which we can return throughout our lives. It is the sacred ground of the soul, where we are naked and can meet ourselves.

Direct inner experience meditation: While sitting, let yourself be. Do not interfere with your thoughts and emotions. Rather, bring your attention to what is going on inside you by scanning your body and being aware of your emotions. Whatever you find, and however upsetting, boring, predictable, peaceful, wild or painful it might be, try to stay quietly focused, without judgment, negations, excitement, or expectations. Be curious and interested in what you find, like a child discovering a flower the first time.

Simply bringing your attention to *what is* takes a lot of practice. Most novices begin by observing their breath, then their thoughts as they come and go—but without getting caught up in the thoughts themselves. If a thought pulls you in, return calmly to the focus of quiet, unattached observation.

If you set this intention—to get into a quiet attitude of focus without attachment to what is going on in your mind and body, you can teach your brain a new habit of returning to this quiet observational place. It will take consistent discipline with daily meditation, but one day, you will find yourself arriving at a place of sudden deeper calm. Breathe in that calm deeper into your body. Consciously enter the calmness, surrender into it, and let it take you up into itself. It will probably quickly disappear the first few times, but, with practice, the calm will stay longer and become more natural-feeling. Eventually, it will come quickly and remain reliably.

With time and practice, the quietude that is innate to this approach will deepen. You may eventually experience that "*it* meditates me," rather than that you are trying to meditate. The first time this happens can be scary because it is so new, but if you stay with it, this fear will pass and the experience will deepen.

Many schools of meditation are based on direct inner experience meditation. Before committing to a teacher, inquire how much are you being asked to "do" and how much are you being shown how to "just be." Go with a school or a teacher that emphasizes the latter. One of the most accessible and reliably well taught is that of vipassana.

Try, for instance, http://www.dhamma.org.

You Meditate How You Eat and Live

Our minds are greatly influenced by what we eat and drink, by the company we keep, and by entertainment, music, and noise. If you are embarking on a spiritual path, consider these influences and consider how you might change them to support your journey. Eating a whole foods diet and healing the digestive system can be helpful before doing profound mental or spiritual work.

White Light for Meditation

My first teacher, Joe Koperski, taught that we should visualize white light rather than imagining a different color for each chakra, for *within the white light, all other colors are present.* He was referring to the laws of physics. These show that when all the colors of light are added together, pure white light results.

In meditating on white light, Joe would say, *any specific color that is needed to bring healing and balance will be extracted by your chakras from the white light.*

However, while some of us can effortlessly imagine white light, it is nearly impossible for others to imagine any luminescence at all. It can be helpful to nudge the imagination by recalling a scene in a movie where white light appears. But if you prefer not to try to see light, that's all right as long as you make an effort to sense and to know that the light is there—let it be an act of faith.

Knowing is Better than Visualizing

Indeed, you do not have to visualize white light at all. Such visualization can be beneficial in the beginning, can help you focus and can generate sensitivity for the healing energies that surround us, but we should be clear that *these are mere mental images.* The light itself is always there in any case. Just as we are surrounded by air and can breathe without thinking about it, we are surrounded by the energy of spirit that sustains us every moment. Simply being cognizant of this while saying the Lord's Prayer and moving through the chakras is enough.

The Meaning of Black

Sometimes, I see no light at all. I may even see a dull grey color, or a rich black darkness. And this is not bad.

My teacher, Appa, who taught direct inner experience meditation, explained that when in meditation we encounter a state or energy that the mind cannot grasp, we will see darkness or get a sense of "nothing being there." That 'nothing' is only 'nothing' because the mind cannot yet identify the 'something' that is there! So if you see only darkness or if you feel as though nothing is happening, do not worry—you may nonetheless be getting in touch with something new, and a part of your mind will explore it and get into closer contact with it if you just stay with it instead of pushing it away saying, "It's nothing, it's just dark."

People tend to be afraid of darkness, associating it with evil. But in meditation, there is no need to be afraid of any dark color. Stay with the intent of the prayer/meditation and you will be fine. There are exceptions, however, that have nothing to do with the darkness itself, but rather to do with the history of the one who is meditating.

Substance Abuse and Trauma

If you are someone who has used a lot of alcohol or drugs, if you have experienced a lot of trauma, or if you have an on-going psychiatric disorder[1] you may find yourself experiencing fearful states during sleep and meditation. These are your own damaged energy states that are knocking on the door of your conscious mind for acceptance, understanding and healing. If you can just "be" with these states, letting the pain and other feelings come into your conscious mind without going out of your center, the feelings will eventually resolve. If you feel overwhelmed by the fear, pain or darkness that you sense in these states, you will need the guidance of a meditation teacher and/or therapist.

Belief in the Devil

Still another exception is in the case of those who believe in the devil and demons, or who went through a time in their lives when they believed in evil spirits looking for any opportunity to enter their energy field and influence them.

My advice: Talk to an experienced teacher of meditation to learn how to deal with these states of darkness and fear when they come up.

---

[1] You might check out SFJane on Youtube; her series explaining how she overcame severe Bi-Polar is very impressive.

3. The White Light Visualization

Joe Koperski's Basic Form

I will present now the basic visualization that I learned from Joseph Koperski in the early 1970s, which forms the basis of the Lord's Prayer Chakra Meditation.

- Sit easily on the floor or chair. If the latter, sit with legs uncrossed, feet flat on the floor, hands on thighs, palms up.
- Breathe deeply and slowly three times.
- Shake your hands gently to release any tension and place them on your thighs again.
- Ask that your mind and heart be open to the vision of the White Light. You can ask now that "Healing White Light," or "Light of Protection," or "Light of Love and Peace" come to you now and enter the room where you are sitting.
- Envision the Light entering your room, rising up from the floor to the ceiling, and filling the room. It is flowing in a spiral motion; it leaves no space unfilled: it lights beneath the furniture, the tables and beds, behind all the furniture and curtains, even in the drawers and closets. The White Light fills the room and penetrates the walls, doors, and windows, filling the corners and pressing up to the ceiling. It is a light of protection and it brings us: peace, love, harmony, balance, self-control, and understanding.
- Breathe deeply and feel the energetic change in the room and around your body. Envision the light circling one inch around your body, from your feet to your head. Envision the light

circling five inches around your body. Now envision the light circling ten inches around your body.

- Feel the closeness of the light, with its peace and love, and feel the release of negative emotions and physical tensions. If you would like, shake your hands gently to release any tension. Imagine that this energy turns into dust.

- To learn how the meditation preparation continues on, read numbers 7-8 on 24-25

Let's Share... Subjective Experience of the Meditation

I am going to share with you how I personally experience the different steps that Joe developed for this meditation.

1. Sitting with the hands open on the thighs allows the energy to flow through us. It is a body position that makes us receptive to new energetic states. When I sit like this, I feel as though I am signaling my mind that I am open for something new.

2. Joe would tell us to inhale and exhale slowly three times. I always feel that this conscious act of breathing moves me into increased receptivity and another state of mind. It's amazing how quickly it happens. The breath contains energy, so-called prana. When we breathe consciously, we take more of this energy into ourselves, and when we consciously intend to move into a more meditative state, the prana prepares and balances our energy bodies for meditation.

3. Shaking the hands is an act of consciously letting go of the emotional and mind state you were in before you sat down to

meditate. When I shake my hands I might imagine letting go of negative things I was holding onto before, or I might just feel that any congestion in my body is now released and I am more able to be "in flow."

4. Joe would call on the light to come into our physical space—the room or building where we were sitting. When you call on the light at any time, it is a kind of invocation, and you might want to make it personal. Name the light something that makes sense to you, or experiment with different names. For instance, ask for the white light of healing, or the white light of protection, the white light of higher self, or for god's sacred white light. Experiment with different names and see if the quality you feel with each is slightly different.

5. Joe would say to imagine that light is entering the room, rising from the floor to the ceiling. I like this image—it prompts my mind to sense the place in which I sit as a three-dimensional space, and this seems to have a sensitizing effect on the nerves of my body and an opening effect on my mind. Imagining light filling the room is accompanied by a sense of relief and renewal, as if I'm suddenly able to let go of worries and emotional burdens. Sometimes though I become aware of dark emotions and burdens that are deep in my body. The light shows me what is there. I no longer suppress it, and I trust that during meditation, these darker states will resolve as much as is possible at this time. I might also become aware of heavy emotional or mental states that are in the room. I know that the white light is resolving this darkness and changing the energetic atmosphere of the building.

23

6. Joe would say that when the light has filled the room, it now surrounds the body. It helps to imagine the light being especially bright a few inches around the body. This image conveys a strong sense of protection. It also moves the mind to sense the three-dimensionality of the body, and to help us get in touch with our physical being. Very often, we perceive our body as if looking in a mirror—we only really *feel* the front of our body. We have no sense for where our backside is—unless something hurts. When the perception of three-dimensionality is trained, the mind becomes more alive and *subtle*—to use a word from yoga for which I can find no better. You can then learn how to "scan" your body—a useful step for direct inner meditation as well, as it tells you immediately "what is."

7. Joe would now have us imagine light concentrated above the head, and then entering into the body through the top of the head in a circular motion. It will travel down to the feet, and then return back to the head. The exact path it follows is: down through the head, filling out the back of the head as well, down through the neck and into the shoulders, relaxing the muscles there, down into the arms, past the elbows and into the hands and fingertips, wait a moment, feel it tingling there, and then return back to the shoulders. Now the light travels down through the trunk of the body, circling the spine, nourishing the organs, and into the hips. It travels down through the legs, into the feet and toes, and out through the feet. Then it returns into the feet, and travels back up through the body into the head, where it stays as you sense the light all over your body. I always feel that as the light goes through the body, I can feel

where it is blocked, or where it encounters tension or repressed feelings. I dwell in those areas until I feel that something has released and cleared up. At times, my neck will involuntarily move in one direction or the other, as if adjusting itself. My spine may do the same; it seems to stretch and straighten up of its own accord. I feel then as though I am younger. My nerves are both activated and relaxed. Joe often said that we were charging our cells—that's what it feels like.

8. Joe advised that whenever we work with white light visualization, we imagine white light moving in a circular motion. He would describe small spirals of white light filling the room, and ask us to imagine the light circling around our bodies. When the light entered the body through the feet, or through the top of the head, it spiraled its way (in a circular motion) through the body as it traveled from one place to the next. I have always practiced the white light visualization with the spiraling, circular motion of light or energy. When I ground myself, I "spiral" my energies down through my head and body into my feet. If I travel with the light from one chakra to the next, I imagine a spiraling, light-filled movement connecting the two chakras. I find the circular motion concept to be very three-dimensional and I believe that this has a beneficial influence on the way that the mind grasps the energetic process that is happening within the body or in the space around me.

Meditation on Joe's Qualities of Light

In his warm, base voice, Joe would lead his ten to thirty regular students in the white light visualization. We would enter the light, expand our chakras and then learn astrology, healing, numerology, and integrate passages and prayers from the Bible into his healing meditations.

Joe's classes began at 7 pm and went to 10 or 11, three evenings a week. It was donation based: everyone gave what they could, whether 2 or 20 dollars. Today, if you want a similar experience, you have to pay thousands of dollars and you still probably won't have it. Fortunately—the experience is within each of us. With commitment and diligence, it can be yours—for free.

Joe would repeat several times during the visualization that we should "Ask that the white light come to us with its qualities of peace, love, harmony, balance, self-control, and human understanding."

The qualities were always the same, but when Joe spoke the words, it was never repetitive or boring. Each word seemed to contain an imprint of the actual thing he was describing. When he said "peace," his voice has a quality to it of vast quietude and sparkling horizons. When he said "love," his voice had warmth and a commitment to it, as if reflecting our sacred contract with god and with the people we encounter in life. When he said "harmony," there was sense in the room of everything in life working together for a greater purpose and joy. "Balance," "self-control," and "human understanding" had to do with the ways that the higher qualities affected our abilities to be centered within ourselves in everyday life.

In the years to come, I would often repeat the qualities that Joe described at the beginning of the Lord's Prayer Chakra meditation, and I would try to recall the feelings I had felt when I actually heard his voice.

Gradually, I understood that the precise order of the qualities had a reason. He began with *peace*, the word that most closely matches the indescribable sense of bliss of higher consciousness. When that bliss becomes part of our human consciousness, it generates an effect on our emotional being: we become open to *love*. When this higher love becomes part of our human consciousness, we begin to make *harmony* a priority—not in that we compromise ourselves for others, but in that we make the needs of all beings our priority so that all beings are served. And this affects our personality so that we now want to live with moderation, (balance, self-control, and human understanding), because without moderation, the qualities of peace, love, and harmony don't have chance to become a manifest part of our lives.

Today, when I recall Joe's qualities, I usually am lying in bed, either going to sleep or waking up. I ask the white light to come into my room and circle around my body with its qualities of...

Peace – I feel a tingling rain of tiniest drops of bliss and peace descending through the light onto my body. It cools, refreshes, transforms.

Love – I feel a cloud of warmth and generosity suffusing my body and mind; a bountiful sense of well being that extends to me and to all beings. It warms, enlivens, encourages.

Harmony – I feel from beneath my body a powerful force that sustains and shows me my place in all things through a sense of rightness and solidarity with all.

Balance – I feel the ability to carefully weigh my choices and my actions, to be moderate in my approach so that my long-term goals are never completely out of sight through the impulse of the moment.

Self-Control – I feel empowered and responsible (responsible = able to respond), aware of the repercussions of my past actions on others and myself, and clear about the actions needed to unfold my positive future plans.

Human Understanding – My thought processes are discerning, logical but also intuitive, flexible, responsive, far-reaching, and compassionate. When we understand truly, we can forgive others and ourselves. Then we can all move forward together.

4.) Before you start the

Lord's Prayer Chakra Meditation...

...there are three concepts to review:

1. The visualization of white light
2. Maintain connection to your body
3. Life and spirit unfold slowly: never force it

1. The visualization of white light

I have written about "seeing" white light on page 18. If you have not yet read this section, do so before continuing.

2. Maintain connection to your body

In order to stay healthy and to function well and enjoy a balanced life, you need a good connection to your body. This connection is much easier to lose than one might imagine. Drugs, alcohol, trauma, lack of sleep and chronic stress or illness can lead to a loss of connection to one's body—as can meditation, fasting, and profound dietary changes.

A word about substance use and abuse: you will not be able to meditate as long as you are using any drug with regularity. Terence McKenna, the late great shamanistic teacher, spoke of getting high *at most* once a year on psychedelic mushrooms. More than that, he said, is counterproductive. I am not advocating using any drugs for spiritual development, but if you choose to do so, know that utmost care has to be taken to keep the use to a minimum.

Even a seemingly harmless drug like marijuana can affect one's connection to the body, reduce one's ability to be focused in daily life, and also to be focused in prayer or meditation. One clairvoyant explained to me that marijuana expands the aura forcibly and rips holes in it. You actually lose your ability to pull your energy body closer to your physical body, and you lose your natural sense of energetic-boundaries for self-protection. This may temporarily bring one a sense of softness, openness, and intuition, even of being temporarily catapulted into a higher state of consciousness, but the negative effects can be considerable. Many people who use marijuana lose the thread of their own lives, become passive or develop serious states of paranoia.

If drugs or alcohol have played a role in your life, your meditations may feel more like vivid daydreams than clear states of awareness. If the use has been considerable, you could experience anxiety, paranoia, helplessness, and a sense of no direction and no connection from day to day. If so, you will need to do some serious bodywork and detoxing to enable your body and mind to be focused and clear.

One sign of how well you are in your body is how well you perceive time. A second is how well you store memories. If you go one day to the next, living on impulse, unable to remember what happened of significance the day or week before, and unable to act on your own plans, you are out of your body and need to make getting back a priority!

I emphasize the problem here because I would not want anyone to use this prayer-meditation in such a way that would exacerbate their problem. My humbly offered advice is this: If you have a loose connection to your body, do the research and rectify the problem before beginning with more intense prayer or meditation.

If you have a good connection to your body, do not take it for granted! In today's world, you are lucky. Work consciously to maintain your body connection. You should feel more in contact with your body, and not less, when you do the Lord's Prayer Chakra Meditation.

Tips for maintaining your body connection:

• Eat well, and get enough sleep.

• Address any metabolic or nutritional issues you have, such as blood sugar imbalances, insulin resistance, food allergies, nutritional deficits, and candidiasis. If you have PMS, read about natural treatments. Look up these terms online to learn more.

• Avoid overuse of stimulants such as caffeine, and use no artificial sweeteners—stevia is okay.

• Cultivate relaxation techniques and deep breathing exercises to help prevent the build-up of stress.

- Learn conflict management techniques. Always take time to think through situations. Wait until you have understood a situation completely, by communicating with everyone involved and by doing the necessary research, before acting.

- When you complete the Lord's Prayer Chakra Meditation, focus on your legs and feet. Feel how your body is energized, and bring the energy into your bones.

- Or complete the meditation by putting your entire focus beneath your feet, and grounding yourself with the earth.

- Wear a hat if you feel your aura is a little "elevated" to help you feel the top of your head and get more of your energy inside your body.

- Feel your feet solidly on the floor when you walk. Feel your bottom on your chair and your feet on the floor when you sit. Know where your spine is.

- Learn and practice a little Qi Gong every day. Of all the body/mind techniques, this is the easiest and the most grounding and balancing.

3. Life and spirit unfold slowly: never force it

In our consumer culture, where we expect quick results, we'd take a pill for enlightenment if we could. This can be a conflict and a conundrum. Spiritual development takes time. Give yourself time.

New insights may inspire and motivate you, but that does not change the fact that *the journey itself is long*. Forcing development may ricochet on you in ways you don't expect. Suddenly changing your lifestyle and diet and job could move you into a new level of development, but it might also leave you feeling disoriented and make you vulnerable to so-called 'spiritual teachers' who just want to attract followers and money.

We may be grown-up biologically, but in terms of a spiritual journey, we are children. When you were a child, you probably felt much more grown up with each year that passed. But with hindsight, it is easy to see that at each age we were still immature in ways that we did not suspect. The same thing with our spiritual maturity: it is a lifetime-project!

Therefore, cultivate a "beginner's mind" toward life and development, and do not be in a hurry. Like the story of the race between the rabbit and the hare, you will probably find that you get to the goal quicker if you go slow but steady and sure.

5. The Basic Lord's Prayer Chakra Meditation

This is a simple rendition of the Lord's Prayer Chakra Meditation that you can memorize or record to listen to while you practice the prayer-meditation. You could also ask someone else to record the prayer-meditation for you. The audiobook edition of this book will also contain meditations such as this one, guided by the author's own voice. A more complex, inner exploration of the phrases follows in Part Two.

After preparing with the basic white light visualization described on pages 21-22, imagine the white light now concentrated above your head. It is going to enter your body through the chakra at the top of your skull and travel down from chakra to chakra in a circular motion, and when you are in each chakra it will also travel in a circular motion around that chakra.

At the top of your head, visualize white light and say, "Our Father (Father-Mother, Source)"

- Go with the light to your forehead and say, "Who art in Heaven"

- Go with the light to your throat and say, "Hallowed be thy Name"

- Go with the light to your heart and say, "Thy Kingdom come"

- Go with the light to your solar plexus, just below the ribs and encompassing the area to below your naval, and say, "Thy Will be Done, on Earth as it is in Heaven.

- Go with the light to your lower abdomen, just above our public bone and say, "Give us this day our daily bread"

- Go with the light to the base of your spine and into your genitals and say, "Forgive us our debts, as we forgive our debtors"

- Go with the light to the muscles of your loins and your thighs and say "And lead us not into temptation"

- Go with the light into your legs and feet and say, "But deliver us from evil"

- Go with the light beneath your feet, and feel yourself grounded on the earth and in your life, and say, "For Thine is the Kingdom, and the Power, and the Glory, forever and ever. Amen."

Part Two

The Light of Christ Consciousness
through the Seven Chakras
and the Human Auric System

1. The Biblical Creation Story in the Lord's Prayer, the Chakras, and the Paths of Life

In this book I try not to write too abstractly, with one exception: The metaphysical symbolism inherent to the biblical creation story as it relates to the first three phrases in the Lord's Prayer, the highest three chakras, and the first three of the life paths. Let us jump into these deep waters and try to swim!

The biblical creation story tells us that the earth was dark in the beginning, without form and void—suggesting that no place, no time, and no differentiation (duality) existed. The Bible goes on to explain that God spoke, and from God's word, or vibration of sound, the universe and the world came into existence, one step, or day, at a time. These Biblical "events" are symbolically paralleled in first three phrases of the Lord's Prayer, in the highest three chakras, and in the first three life paths of astrology.

ONE – In the Lord's Prayer, we first address what might be called God's divine essence with the words: "Our Father." This entity we commonly call "God" exists beyond what language can describe, but we use language to direct our mind towards it. We address it.

In its pure essence, without form and void, "God's" existence at this point seems to be very much like the Buddhist "nothingness" or the Hindu "Original Ocean of Being" that was before all things and always will be. The first utterance of the Hindu entity Purusha—the divine Self that pervades the universe—is: "I am." God said to Moses when asked for a name: "I am that I am." Here, at the very beginning and beyond time and place, God is pure essence and therefore cannot be named.

> We address the "I am" when we say: "Our Father."[2]"

- Bible: The Void – or pure, indescribable 'being;' "I am"
- We say: Our Father – We address the *essential abstract all-pervasive being* commonly called God
- Bible: God's Manifestation as Creator –God becomes more describable, has the attributes of a Creator
- We say: Who Art in Heaven – God's *form and place* are established, God is less abstract than in the first phrase
- Bible: God's Word is spoken– the spiritual, creative power of sound and intention is established.
- We say: Hallowed be thy Name – *The Word* that identifies God shall be held sacred: we state our intention, to revere the name or sound we associate with God.

TWO – "Who Art in Heaven." God takes on definition. Although the ultimate "I am" exists beyond geography, we designate God a place, not concretely on earth, but in heaven, a concept that is less abstract than the pure "I am." Here we indulge our need to imagine or conceive of God as form—as a bearded old man in the clouds, perhaps, or some other *image*. Indeed, when

---

[2] We could also say, "Our Mother," "Our Source," "Our Highest Self," etc.

we study the correlations with the chakras, this phrase of the prayer corresponds to the chakra where we create high mental images. We require these mental constructs in order to imagine and to pray (in contrast to meditation, where no mental construct is necessary, even if it comes from a higher chakra).

> We draw the abstract concept of God closer to us through the mental construct of a geography of heaven. We give God the job of a quasi-ruler over that ultimate "Kingdom."

THREE – We say, "Hallowed be Thy Name." With this phrase we acknowledge that God is mysteriously linked to a vibrational pattern, to *sound*, to the mystery of language and thus to a name. The so-called "Name of God," whatever that might be in whichever belief system, is revered, chanted, prayed, and held sacred. Furthermore, taking the name of god in vane—that is, using it for one's own ambitions, as would a corrupt priest or any manipulative, self-serving so-called 'religious person'—is considered a major and unforgivable sin in both the East and West.

The concept of a sacred sound-bridge (God's Name or other sound that symbolizes God) between God's essence and human language is universal. As a parallel, God's creational power in the Bible is referenced as "God's Word." In Eastern religions, the sound "Om" is designated as the creational sound of the universe, and it is reported that one may hear this sound in deep meditation. Conversely, chanting "Om" can bring the mind into harmony with a spiritual state and is therefore a common way to begin meditation.

> The Name of God is holy. This refers to the mystery of language and to the sound-bridge that emanates from God in the act of creation, and that, conversely, as a sound in our mind and language, links us back to God's sacred essence.

We've now briefly looked at the way that the language of the first three phrases of the Lord's Prayer mirrors the creation myth of the Bible and other religions: **Our Father** "I am," **In Heaven** "Mind-Image or Spiritual Identity," **Hallowed be thy name** the sacred mystery of consecrated sound or God's Word/Name in all cultures.

Now let us look into the correlations between the creation story, the Lord's Prayer, and the chakras.

- God/ (God as Essence) – Seventh Chakra at top of head
- Heaven/Thought-World (God as Image, as thought form) – Sixth Chakra at the forehead
- Word/Language (God as Sound) – Fifth Chakra at the throat

Each chakra represents a unique state of consciousness. At the top and just above the head, the **seventh** "Crown Chakra" connects us with a pure spiritual quality or state that is said to be beyond description—that means, beyond words. Any attempt to define the experience of this state is futile because words themselves have an exclusive quality (something is this and not that, true or false, black or white) that prevents the all-inclusiveness of the experience from being captured.

Words like suchness, thatness, bliss, non-dual, Christ-Consciousness, nirvana, satori, nothingness or "being one with everything" can only hint at the experience.

Thus, the first phrase of the Lord's Prayer corresponds to the seventh chakra that connects us to the blissful state of pre-creation, pre-mind, pre-language.

The **sixth** chakra, localized within the skull behind the forehead, is where we create our concepts and images. It is where we experience inspirations, insights, intuitions, and where we conceive the ideal. Whereas in the seventh chakra we experience ourselves as one with everything, but cannot put that experience into words, here we are in the higher mental and able to create in an inner geography of "heaven," populated by our most elevated mental constructs.

> Thus, the second phrase of the Lords' Prayer, in which God is placed within the geography of heaven, corresponds to the geography-of-concept that is inherent to the sixth chakra.

In the sixth chakra, we are in contact with the divine through inspiration, but we can also become very attached to our higher mentality and not realize that there is something beyond its parameters.

The **fifth** chakra, localized within the throat/neck, corresponds to our more personal ideas—not to our greater scope of concepts, ideals and inspirations, that are indigenous to the sixth chakra, but to thoughts about everyday life and about the world and universe in which we live. This is the chakra of language and communication, as well as of secret thoughts, plans, intrigues, etc.

> Thus, the third phrase of the Lord's Prayer, in which we bow to the mystery of language and to the sacred nature of God's name, corresponds to the chakra of language.

Finally, let's look ever so briefly at the correlations between the creation story, the Lord's Prayer, and the first three of the 12 life paths.

In astrological terms, these first paths correspond to the first three division of the Zodiac, and are the signs of Aries, Taurus, and Gemini. The essences of these three divisions are:

- Aries – Self ("I am")
- Taurus – Place/Form ("I have")
- Gemini – Language ("I speak")

If you have been following along this far, the correlations will now jump out at you.

We have here the same movement from Self ("I am"), through Form (Heaven), to Name (mystery of language or sacred sound-bridge).

The first three phrases of the Lord's Prayer, the three highest chakras and the first three Paths correlate in a way that hopefully now appears clear.

On pages 44–57 you will find a concise description of the correlations between the individual phrases of the Lord's Prayer and the chakras, followed by a brief description of the correlations between the phrases of the Lord's Prayer and the 12 life paths. This will be discussed in detail in Part Two.

On pages 58–83 you will find the very heart of this book – a more in-depth exploration of the prayer-chakra correlations.

2. The Seven Chakras

1) **Top of the skull, the 7th chakra.** Beyond mental. Pure bliss of consciousness, absence of any sense of the personal 'I'. Non-dual. Here we encounter the vibrational quality of Oneness, Source and bliss.

2) **Center of forehead, the 6th chakra.** Higher Mental. Here the personal 'I' identifies with Source, and we have a 'spiritual I' or mental abode where concepts of spirituality can unfold. Inspiration, intuition, ideals.

3) **The throat, the 5th chakra.** Lower mental. Here we experience personal thoughts, ideas, plans, secrets, and we build mental constructs of duality such as good and evil, god and devil, higher and lower, light and darkness.

4) **Heart center, 4th chakra.** The higher mid-point between spiritual energy and earth energy. It is said that this is where the true "spiritual I" resides, the true home of Source within the body/mind/aura. It is important to cultivate this chakra at the onset and throughout one's spiritual journey.

Corresponding Phrases

1) *Our Mother / Father / Source* – We address our own Pure Being, the "I am" state of blissful consciousness at the 7th chakra at the top of the head.

2) *In Heaven* – Pure Being takes on form, is 'in heaven' - an identifiable though fully abstract 'place.' This is the highest mental realm, that corresponds to the 6th chakra at the forehead.

3) *Hallowed be Thy Name* – Pure Being is named. The sound of name builds a bridge from the human mind to the divine. This is in the lower mental of the 5th chakra. We ask that within the realm of our lower thoughts, we always think of spirit with full respect.

4) *Thy Kingdom Come* – Pure Being is centered in the heart, the energetic home of Spiritual Source in the aura, at the 4th chakra. We ask that spirit make our heart its home.

5) **Solar Plexus, 3rd chakra**. This is the lower mid-point between spiritual energy and earth energy. Whereas the heart center links up to spiritual being, the 3rd chakra of will is usually directed toward the earth environment. Aligning one's personal will with one's spirit source is an ongoing process in spiritual development—the 3rd and 4th chakras develop into one strong, centered, loving and empowering direction.

6) **Lower abdomen, 2nd chakra**. This chakra metabolizes earth energy and represents our interconnectedness with other human beings and the planet. We live as an interdependent being within an earth community. Wrong action creates spiritual debt and emotional guilt, and can endanger physical health, mental stability, and the well being of the community.

7) **Base of the spine, 1st chakra**. This chakra is most closely connected to our animal nature, to desires, greed, sexuality and reproduction, but also to dormant spiritual energy. Here we might injure others for selfish reasons, or act self-destructively (karmic debt).

Corresponding Phrases

5) *Your Will be done, on Earth as in Heaven* – Pure Being enters the emotional-energetic state of the 3rd chakra, where pure earth energy is metabolized into Will and Creativity for culture and change on earth. When you say this phrase in this chakra, you send an impulse to align your forces of will with your spiritual purpose.

6) *Daily Bread* – Pure Being willingly accepts the need to work to feed oneself and ones family and community. This is the energy of the 2nd chakra, that has to do with accepting inter-dependency without becoming co-dependent.

7) *Forgive us our debts, as we forgive our debtors* – Here Pure Being acknowledges that we live in a community with others, and how we are bound to live together through ethical considerations, community laws, and karmic debts and commitments.

8) **The Loins, also 1st and 2nd Chakras.** Sexual desires are especially imprinted into the muscles that we call the loins, powerful muscles that flank the hips and upper thighs. This muscular area encircles the lower two chakras. This is where we physically act on desire, and it is a metaphor as well for the most basic decisions we make. We tend to think of desire, greed, and aggression as "bad" but these attributes enable us to exist and survive in a physical body. In addition, we all learn through these basic experiences. The Lord's Prayer aligns the lower chakras with spirit.

9) **The Legs and Feet, downward-directed energy flow and feet chakras.** From the 1st chakra, an energy funnel connects us downward to the earth. This connection also takes place through the legs and feet, and this connection is a metaphor for our path in life and how we travel it. Being receptive to wisdom and guidance is necessary on a spiritual path. Otherwise, we go around in circles.

10) **To complete the prayer,** bring the final three affirmations and celebratory statements into your energy field in one of the ways that is described on pages 80-83.

Corresponding Phrases

8) *Lead us Not into Temptation* – Here Pure Being acknowledges that desire can lead to the heights of wisdom, but along the way will lead us through valleys of darkness. We ask for guidance in the school of desire, that we learn what the different desires, yearnings and longings stem from and what they lead to, so that we can learn discrimination and continue to develop and not get stuck on our life path.

9) *Deliver Us from Evil* – Here Pure Being focuses on deliverance from the down-pulling forces of our own earth-nature, so that we are not short-sighted, bent on desire-satisfaction, but far-sighted, able to comprehend consequences and cultivate values, and so that we can respond to wise teachings and leadership, and later, provide teaching and leadership to others.

10) *For Yours is the Kingdom* – Here Pure Being reaffirms the human society we build together is ultimately one that must evolve to meet the needs of whole, spiritual human beings. It must project out from the spiritual heart.

11) *Yours is the Power* – Here we acknowledge that power on earth stems from knowledge, and that it should be used for the good of all. When we make the welfare of everyone our own concern, we are linked into the energy of Source.

12) *Yours is the Glory* – Here we acknowledge that the deepest level of our spiritual experience where feelings of deep gratitude and devotion and of closeness to spirit are our reward, is one and the same as what we call, in an old-fashioned way, 'Glory.'

On the following six pages is a brief description of the correspondences between the 12 paths and the Lord's Prayer, so that the interested reader can delve into these interconnections in one flow here. Explanations follow in Part Three.

3. The Twelve Paths

1) *Aries - I am.* "I am that I am" — without question. I live from the feeling of having an unending source of energy.

2) *Taurus - I have.* I take on form. I enter into and am concerned with the material side of existence. I forget that my nature is pure spirit and become very attached to beauty in form.

3) *Gemini - I think.* Some say, "I speak." I conceptualize, name, communicate. I connect through words and describe the world. The journalist, traveler, tradesperson.

4) *Cancer - I feel.* I connect through my senses with everything. Intuitively, I understand. Through concentrated feeling, I open the door to my spiritual heart center. The mother, nurse, community organizer.

5) *Leo - I will.* I create through my will and my intentions. Some artists, actors, musicians, gamblers.

Corresponding Phrases

1) *Our Mother / Father / Source* – We turn our attention and reverence toward our own Pure Being, the "I am" state of blissful consciousness of being one with everything at the 7th chakra.

2) *In Heaven* – Pure Being takes on form, is 'in heaven.' This corresponds to the 6th chakra. Self-identity as a spiritual being. But not in pure bliss. The beginning of ego.

3) *Hallowed be your Name* – Pure Being is conceptualized and named. In our thoughts and communication, may we always regard spirit with reverence. 5th chakra at the throat.

4) *Your Kingdom Come* – The energetic home of Source in the body and aura is at the heart, the 4th chakra. Ramana Maharishi gives this chakra as the focus for meditation on self.

5) *Your Will be done, on Earth as in Heaven* – Pure Being enters the emotional-energetic state of the 3rd chakra, at the solar plexus, where intention and creativity are seated. These can be thought energies, or pure will power.

6) *Virgo - I work.* Also, "I analyze." I bring myself fully into life, with my energy and my ability to plan, so that I can provide food and shelter for myself and my community. The accountant, biologist, or anyone who brings great attention to detail in their work.

7) *Libra - I judge.* Also, "I balance." I live communally under common laws. The judge, the legislator, the town gossip.

8) *Scorpio - I desire.* I long for extreme experiences and I seek fulfillment. Through sexual pleasure, I regenerate myself and procreate.

Corresponding Phrases

6) *Daily Bread* – Pure Being acknowledges the need to work to feed oneself and one's family and community, accepting inter-dependency without becoming co-dependent. 2nd chakra just above pubic area, metabolizing of intra-human experiences.

7) *Forgive us our debts, as we forgive our debtors* – here Pure Being acknowledges community life and laws, ethical considerations, and karmic debts and commitments. 1st chakra at the base of the spine, where, in one aspect, one's plan of life is laid out in the form of karmic debts to resolve.

8) *Lead us not into temptation* – Here Pure Being acknowledges that desire can lead to great works and wisdom, but initially, it may lead us through valleys of darkness. We ask for guidance in the school of desire, so that we can learn discrimination and continue to grow. Second aspect of 1st chakra – extreme experience: sexuality, kundalini energy, reproduction, death.

9) *Sagittarius - I lead.* Also, "I see," "I understand." I study higher learning, I understand subtle aspects of life, I perceive far-reaching consequences. Therefore, I can lead others. The philosopher, teacher, priest.

10) *Capricorn - I build.* Another form is "I use." I construct structures for society's future, such as institutions and politics that affect the world. The lawyer, the politician, the CEO.

11) *Aquarius - I know.* The individualist who seeks to expand knowledge for the good of humanity. The inventor. The altruist.

12) *Pisces - I believe.* Compassionate. I am filled with awe and gratitude for the gift of life, and return deep devotion to the spirit source. The artist. The Mystic. The poet. The intuitive scientist.

Corresponding Phrases

9) *Deliver Us from Evil* – Here Pure Being focuses on deliverance from the down-pulling forces of our own earth-nature, so that we are not short-sighted, bent on desire-satisfaction, but far-sighted, able to comprehend conesquences and cultivate values, and so that we can respond to wise teachings and leadership, and later, provide teaching and leadership to others.

10) *For Yours in the Kingdom* – Here we affirm that the human society we build together is ultimately one that must evolve to meet the needs of developing spiritual human beings. Our plans must project from the spiritual heart.

11) *Yours is the Power* – Here we affirm that the greatest power on earth is that of caring. When we care, when we make the welfare of everyone our own concern, we are linked into the force of Source.

12) *Yours is the Glory* – Here we affirm that reverence, or gratitude and devotion towards God, is necessary to being a complete human being. We call this here in churchy language: 'Giving God the Glory.'

7.

Chakra: The Seventh Chakra
Body Part: Top of Head
Prayer Part: "Our Father"
Path of Life: "I am"

The Meditation begins...

The meditation begins by sensing, acknowledging or visualizing light at the top of the head, and then beginning the prayer with the first phrase.

Speak into this chakra: "Our Father."

But you should know that in the original prayer, which was written in Aramaic, the word for God did not represent the Father alone, but also the Mother. It is a word for the complete God, Father and Mother, and also Source.

If you feel inclined, you can say "Our Father-Mother," "Our Mother," "Our Father," or, "Our Source."

Say whatever is right for you, and that helps connect you to the beauty, intimacy and joy inherent in the relationship to God. If you do not have a positive feeling toward either your father or mother, this could be difficult. But simply saying this opening phrase with concentration at the top of head, or the chakra that connects us with source, provides an impulse for our relationship to Source and Creator to be healed.

This then is the healing potential in the seventh chakra: We heal our relationship to Source, and we begin healing and our relationship with our own mother and father.

Here I would like to mention that when we talk about the 12 paths of astrology, the path of life that corresponds to this chakra and to "Our Father/Mother/Source" is:

The Path of "Being."
The person on this path says, "I am," (and don't you dare contradict me).

Or, as the Biblical God pronounces, "I am that I am."
And, as Christ says, "I am the Light."

Thus, in the seventh chakra, God/Source/Self is.

And is perfect.

And we are one with ourselves and with the spiritual nature of ALL and EVERYTHING here.

6.

Chakra: The Sixth Chakra
Body Part: Forehead
Prayer Part: "Who Art in Heaven"
Path of Life: "I have."

The meditation continues...

Travel with the light to your forehead. This is the place of the sixth chakra. My teacher Appa used to say that this is the place where we experience our spiritual self-identity. This is where our aspiration takes shape as an image. That image could be an idealized, spiritualized being—a subtle spiritual ego-trip...

"I am so great because I am so spiritual."

But it can also be where we have deeper spiritual insights and intuitions that link us to our spirit.

This is, indeed, where we give the spiritual in us "space" as a concept or image. This is where we conceive of Heaven. This is where God, or our own God-Self, takes on form.

The seventh and the sixth chakras are closely related energetically, though one is a state of formless consciousness, and the other takes on the form of concepts. In one, we find bliss that is so abstract and overwhelming that the mind cannot grasp it. In the other, the mind creates a beautiful image of the god-self.

While concentrating on your forehead, say:

"Who Art in Heaven."

God exists—abstract, incomprehensible—and the mind creates a Heaven for God. We have given God a home beyond earth, but a home nonetheless.

Now, when we talk about the 12 paths of Astrology, the Path that correlates to this chakra, and to this phrase of the prayer, "Who art in heaven," is:

The Path of "Place," and "Possession," symbolized by the Bull, with his hooves dug into the earth, positioned in a steady stance.

The person on this path says, "I have" (and don't you dare take it from me.

I have stuff. I am in the process of gathering material possessions around my being. I am no longer purely abstract, but am taking form.

5.

Chakra: The Fifth Chakra

Body Part: Throat and mouth

Prayer Part: "Hallowed be thy name."

Path of Life: "I Speak"

The meditation continues...

Now let the sense of light flow down through your head and into your neck. The fifth chakra is in your throat, and is linked to the mouth and to language. The energy of this chakra allows concepts to be expressed. Here we find our inner library of words and thoughts, and an archive of memories. But here we also archive thoughts we wouldn't want to share with anyone else: secret thoughts, sneaky plans, and other things (Appa used to say, our mental library of porn videos). This is the so-called 'back of the mind.'

We are now at the chakra where we express ourselves, and where we also articulate our spiritual nature. The shadow side of the fifth chakra relates to sides of ourselves that are not integrated well into our personality, and the resulting thoughts and hurtful words we would rather keep hidden.

Concentrate on your throat chakra and say the words: "Hallowed be Thy Name."

In saying these words, you harmonize your ability to conceptualize, think and articulate with your deepest nature. This nature wishes that everything you say, whether to yourself in the privacy of your mind, or publicly to others, be thought or said in honor of life and in honor of spirit.

In saying these words of the Lord's Prayer into this chakra, you give this chakra an impulse and a guideline.

Do not say this phrase and then feel bad about the way you usually think and speak. This meditation is not about regret and guilt. Rather, say the phrases in trust that the prayer will, over the course of your lifetime, have a deep influence on your patterns of thought and speech.

What you are doing is allowing the experiences of the crown chakra—the energy you experience at the top of your head and at your forehead—to carry over to your experience of yourself as a thinking and expressing human being. And in the same way, these higher energies will travel down to all your chakras and adjust and align them with the spiritual impulses inherent to the prayer—impulses that reflect our true nature.

Here I would like to mention that when we talk about the 12 star paths, the Path that corresponds to the fifth chakra and to the phrase of the prayer "Hallowed be thy name" is:

The Path of Language, symbolized by the Twin Siblings. The person on this path says, "I speak." But the path also corresponds to the perception and description of things seen, processed spoken about in every day life.

4.

Chakra: The Forth Chakra

Prayer Part: "Thy Kingdom come."

Body Part: Heart, center of chest

Path of Life: "I feel."

The meditation continues...

Now follow the light as it travels down through your shoulders into your chest, at your spiritual heart center. When this chakra develops and vibrates intensely, you will feel joy, compassion, love, and confidence.

The heart chakra is where we feel perfectly one with ourselves and with all of life on a fine, emotional level. Here we truly bond with those we love. These bonds, and the way that these bonds deeply affect our emotional life, are held in the heart center. So, while the heart center offers the promise of joy and a compassionate, generous communal bond with our dearest ones and with all of life, what we often feel here is the opposite: grief, loss, and isolation because the bonding experiences we have had with family and friends may not have been positive and supportive.

Mentally say the words into this chakra, "Thy Kingdom Come."

What we do with these words is to give an impulse to the heart center to make the laws and behavior spirit the same laws that govern the way we interact with others and with all of life. We look forward to the time when spiritual energy has brought peace and love to this center, healing, happiness, and a resolution to personal pain. We look forward to being able to form healthy bonds and to having a fulfilling emotional life in a community of vibrant friends and family.

Here I would like to mention that when we talk about the 12 star paths of astrology, the path of this chakra and this phrase of the prayer is:

The Path of Home, symbolized by the Crab. The person on this path says, "I feel."

Indeed, the Heart Center is our true Home—for the home is where the heart is. Our ability to feel and to think with the heart is our true compass in life.

When this chakra receives this impulse, and we commit to God's Kingdom coming to the realm of our heart, we then begin to be rooted in our spiritual home.

3.

Chakra: The Third Chakra

Prayer Part: "Thy will be done."

Body Part: Solar Plexus

Path of Life: "I will."

The meditation continues...

Follow the light down below your ribcage into the area of the solar plexus, called the center of will.

When you feel a powerful desire or determination to do something, the energy of will concentrates itself here. Our "will power" is indiscriminate. That means, it will focus on anything we turn our mind to, whether positive or negative, good or bad, kind or harmful.

This center feels powerful. We feel strong here. It is here that we build our self-esteem—but only if we don't fall flat on our face by making bad decisions based on willing something that is wrong for us or others.

Some of us are the opposite: crippled in our will power. Injuries from childhood play a role. Having been victimized may have left us feeling as though we have no power at all. Another cause: we may have made big mistakes in the past with our will that haunt us. Appa used to say that when we misuse our power and fall on our faces, we are reluctant to use it again. We block ourselves from the get-go, deny ourselves the expression of the third chakra.

Feel your way into this part of your body, and into the energy of the chakra at the solar-plexus. You may feel that you are full of will, that you have very little will, that your will is crippled, or that you have none at all. No matter.

Now say these words into the chakra:

"Thy Will Be Done."

These words give an impulse to this center to align itself with your higher will and with your higher being. It gives an impulse of healing and energizing to this center.

Here I would like to mention that when we talk about the 12 paths of astrology, the path of this chakra and this phrase of the prayer is:

The Path of Will, symbolized by the Lion. The person on this path says, "I will."

In the Lord's Prayer, we say, "Thy Will Be Done," followed by "On Earth as it is in Heaven." The Will is a center for action that is suspended between Heaven and Earth. Eventually, your will power will be attuned to your higher impulses rather than your lower. You don't have to worry about it, you can depend on it—if you continue to give this impulse to this chakra.

2.

Chakra: The Second Chakra

Prayer Part: "Give us our daily bread"

Body Part: Reproductive Organs, intestines

Path of Life: "I work."

Meditation continues...

When you are ready, let the light settle down deeper into your torso. At the base of your abdomen, just above your pubic bone, is the second chakra. It is involved in your physical metabolic processes such as the absorption and digestion of food, and the health of your sexual organs. Here we experience the existential aspect of physical life—eat or die. Here we metabolize food into energy, and expel it as waste products. Here we create semen, or we carry a baby in our womb.

Here say the words:

"Give us this day our daily bread."

The prayer refers us to an attitude about life. We must eat, and that means that we must work. So, "daily bread" refers not primarily to food, but rather to the toil we must accept and fulfill if we are to eat. The prayer suggests an attitude: please give us the opportunity to work for our food. We do not wish to starve. We would rather work than starve, and we would rather be grateful for the opportunity to work than resentful that we must work.

If we do not like the work we do but have no other option, why waste the precious time of life being caught up in hateful emotions about it?

A humble attitude toward the work required to survive can help us fulfill the demands of everyday life with an accepting mind and with gratitude. It can correct congested emotional blockages typically found in this chakra. *tj pɪ kᵈ/i*

This chakra, that relates more than any other to where and how we stand in life, is where we carry our shame. It is where we hold long-standing emotions towards people who have hurt us, as well as towards those we have hurt. These energies travel upwards and affect our heart center with emotional pain, and cloud our upper centers with guilt and mental compulsions. On the level of the second chakra, these emotions can interfere in our body's metabolism of food. We may be constipated, have irritable bowel syndrome, develop food sensitivities, or feel weak and have a reduced immune system.

Feel your way into this center, and mentally speak these words of humility and acceptance: "Give us this day our daily bread."

Here I would like to mention that when we talk about the 12 paths of astrology, the path of this chakra and this phrase of the prayer is:

The Path of Employment, symbolized by the Goddess of the Harvest. The person on this path says, "I work."

ha: vɪsf

69

1.

Chakra: The first chakra

Prayer Part: "Forgive us our debts, as we forgive our debtors."

Body Part: Reproductive Organs

Path of Life: "I balance, I judge."

The Meditation Continues...

This phrase of the Lord's Prayer addresses the first chakras' function as an archival place of debt and karma.

Follow the light as it settles into the base of your spine. Just before in section 2, I mentioned that we hold congested emotions about people we have hurt or who may have hurt us in the second chakra. But Appa used to say that the *record* of personal debt to others, or incurring someone's debt to us, is stored deep within the first chakra as the seeds of karma.

Thus, this statement, "Forgive us our debts, as we forgive our debtors," spoken deeply into the first chakra, brings an impulse for release of debt—both our debt to others, and debt that is still owed to us. This is the essence of Christianity: forgiveness for everyone, so that we can all move forward together on a spiritual journey.

What we call debt or sin in western traditions is called karma in eastern traditions. But what is karma? In simplest terms, it means that what goes around comes around.

Karma is the stuff of our lives. Everyone has a mix of good and bad karma, depending on the choices we make at many crossroads of our lives.

Because today we live in a toxic world, most of us are indeed still, affected with physical or emotional illness or with both. In this sense, we all participate in a kind of world-karma. The sins of the fathers are visited on the sons, and of the mothers on the daughters. The debt of wrong choices is passed on from generation to generation.

Now feel your way into this first center and say:

"Forgive us our debts, as we forgive our debtors."

These words bring an impulse to move calmly towards the resolution of debts, on an individual level, as a culture, and as part of the world community.

Here I would like to mention that when we talk about the 12 paths of astrology, the Path of this chakra and this phrase of the prayer correspond to:

The Path of Justice, symbolized by the Scales of Justice. The person on this path says, "I balance, but also, I judge."

1a.

Chakra: The first chakra, another aspect
Prayer Part: "Lead us not into temptation"
Body Part: Loins, groin, upper thighs, flanks
Path of Life: "I desire."

The meditation continues...

In contrast to the last section that addressed this chakra's role as the recorder of karmic debt, this phrase of the Lord's Prayer addresses this chakras' function as a portal to the "other side." Here we experience aspects of human-being that go far beyond our normal consciousness and bring us to the "threshold:" sex, procreation, regeneration, being born, dying, sleep, meditation, and deeply transformative experiences.

Travel with the light into the flanks of your hips and into your upper thighs, also called the *loins* and the *groin*. The "fruit of the loins" is a metaphor for children. These strong muscles form a protective structure around the first and second chakras. These muscles carry us upright through everyday life. They enable us to walk, to propel the physical body through space. But these same muscles are also active in sex and in childbirth.

This chakra connects us down through our legs to pure earth energy in the same way that the crown chakra connects us to pure spirit energy. Thus, its role as a portal. It is here that we experience the ecstasy of sexuality—where we regenerate energetically and emotionally through orgasm. Here we sink into regenerative sleep, or into transformative meditation. Through this chakra we allow a human soul to take on physical form through our genetic resources and by sharing our body space. It is thus a portal in this sense as well, and gives us the opportunity to participate in the miracle of life and death.

The shadow side of this chakra occurs when a person is unable to respond to the impulse for transformation. "Control freaks" are typically afraid of transformation because to truly transform it is necessary, and if only for a moment, to give up the sense of being in control. For instance, many people suffer from insomnia and bad dreams. To enter deep, restful sleep requires an essential level of trust; we have to "let go." Not everyone is able to experience orgasm for the same reason.

People who do not have basic trust often develop some degree of obsessive-compulsive disorder (OCD), destructive behavior towards self or other, and/or enter an addictive pattern. Most people today have some degree of OCD. That speaks volumes about how we live, how little we trust, and about our relationship to our first chakra and to earth energy.

To have transformative and regenerative experiences, it is not necessary to trust and surrender to a god, or to a sexual partner. Transformative powers lie within our own being. They are rooted in our "root chakra." If we tap into them, we can begin to heal.

At this point in the Lord's Prayer-meditation, we go into the muscles surrounding our hips that extend down into the thighs.

We speak the words: Lead us not into temptation.

This is the first "negative" sounding phase of the Lord's Prayer. All the others are positive and affirming. I believe this negativity reflects our tumultuous fears about the experiences inherent to this chakra.

In some versions of the Lord's Prayer, the words ""And go with us into temptation" are spoken instead. Say these words into your first chakra and see how they resonate there.

But, what is temptation, and would God lead us there, or go with us there?

When we think of temptation, we usually mean either a misuse of power or a 'mistake' we make, due to the desires of the flesh.

The two concepts are closely tied.

For the desire for power usually stems from an obsessive compulsive and unreflected desire to resist the transformative energies of life. We strive to sit at the top of some kind of industry where we command respect and play god over other people's lives. But this is just a distraction. We are distracting ourselves from what we have come here to do, which is to grow more solidly as a whole human being. Thus, when we follow temptation, regardless of the kind of temptation, we are distracted from our deeper purpose.

But would God lead us into temptation?

Yes. For if life is a school, most of us only learn some lessons through mistakes. Then we alienate ourselves from our higher being. With luck, we begin to suffer inwardly and eventually come to understand that we have gone off our path. We come to understand what our deeper desires and deeper purpose truly are, what our life's path should look like.

This chakra links our energy body into our legs through the strong muscles of the hips. Well, we rely on our legs in an unconscious, trusting way. When we get up from bed in the morning, we do not wonder whether our legs will hold us. We walk, all day, from here to there and back again.

Our personal path of life is thus symbolized by the legs. The act of walking represents the act of making choices and taking decisions as to where we want to go and how we plan to get there. Along the way, all of us have moral decisions to make that involve possibly hurting or exploiting others, including hurting or exploiting the earth environment.

All of us do, at times, make bad decisions. We will fall into temptation, into forgetfulness of what is real and valuable. We fall into self-delusion.

And so, in this prayer that calls out to God for help every aspect of our life and being, we implore: "Please go with us on our path of life, and when we make mistakes and fall asleep, wake us up again."

Try speaking these words into this chakra and see how it resonates for you:

"And go with us into temptation."

"And lead us not into temptation."

To summarize, this chakra corresponds to sex and to physical reproduction, but also to experiences of spiritual death and rebirth, and to processes of metamorphosis within the course of our lives. Indeed, if we successfully allow life to transform us into more mature human beings—by making mistakes and learning from them—we may look back at our lives in old age with the sense that we lived many distinct lives, each with its own set of lessons, and each with its own value.

When I was a kid òf sixteen, a similar aged friend said, "I want to be free to do what I want."

I thought about it and said, "I would be content just to actually know what I want."

Knowing what your higher nature wants is the key to transformation by desire. To begin, know that you are held lovingly in the secure arms of your own deepest being.

Here I would like to mention that when we talk about the 12 paths of astrology, the path of this chakra and this phrase of the prayer correspond to:

The Path of Death and Rebirth, symbolized by the Scorpio and the Eagle. The person on this path says, "I desire."

0. – The connection to earth

Chakra: The energy flowing through the legs into the feet

Prayer Part: "Deliver us from evil."

Body Part: Lower Body, Calves and feet

Path of Life: "I learn, I teach, I lead."

[kaɪvz]

The meditation continues...

The vision of light flows down into the calves and feet. (Small chakras are at the base of the feet.) Here we go more deeply into our legs, and into our path in life, and how we travel that path— the absentminded meanderings, the roads or the alleys, and our attitudes and fears about the course of our life.

Feel your way into your legs and feet and say the words: "And deliver us from evil."

The *conclusion* of the prayer then, is an expression of hope that our life be good. We do not want to be waylaid by temptation, but when we are pulled in by it, we wish to be delivered from it again.

"Delivered" means to be woken up, reminded, perhaps even by personal tragedy, about what we really value in life and what we hope to do here on earth from our deepest heart.

With this phrase of the prayer, we implore God: "Please, do not let me waste time! I know I've got a lot to learn on this earth, and that these lessons will include encounters with illusion, exploitation, bullying, violence, abuse and much more. But let me

77

always come back to my central purpose. Let me be delivered back to my higher being.

I say "the conclusion" of the prayer because the older and earlier version of the Lord's Prayer actually ends with this phrase.

Thus, it thus ends in the calves and feet. And with the feet, we run home again. We are the prodigal son, returning to the arms of his father. We are Persephone, ascending from Hades' realm to the arms of her mother. We are delivered from evil, that is, from temptation and from our own wrong choices. We run home as fast as we can to where we are safe and accepted and forgiven—into the arms of our own higher being.

And with phrase, we have now traveled throughout the entire body and energy system. We have taken Christ Consciousness impulses from our higher self, found in the energy of the seventh chakra, and led it down through all our chakras. We have spoken impulses from each phrase of the prayer into its corresponding chakra, bringing alignment and healing.

We have also addressed the first nine paths of life as described in the astrological divisions of the Zodiac. However, a later form of the prayer added three more phrases, as if on purpose, to complete the 12 paths of astrology. I'll discuss the last three phrases briefly in the next section.

Here I would like to mention that when we talk about the 12 paths of astrology, this chakra and this phrase of the Lord's Prayer correspond to:

The Path of Philosophy and Higher Learning, symbolized by the Centaur (Man's Torso on a Horse Body, holding a bow and arrow). The person on this path says, "I understand," and "I lead."

This is the path of maturity of mind, achieved by using discrimination on the path of life. This is the mentor or the priest, who leads others to more understanding and maturity as well.

The shadow side is intellectual pride. No matter how much we know, and now much we benefit others through our knowledge, we must remember to consider our small place in the way of things, and that we always need to remind ourselves with the phrase, "Deliver us from evil."

10th, 11th, 12th *phrases of the Lord's Prayer*

The Meditation Continues...

As mentioned above, the original Lord's Prayer as found in the books of Mathew and Luke ends with the last phrase, "But deliver us from evil." It thereby encompasses the physical body and the energy system perfectly.

However, later authors of the New Testament thought it good to continue the prayer for three more phrases, bringing the entire number from nine to twelve. Thus, we have twelve phrases that correspond perfectly with the twelve star paths—discussed in more detail in Part Two of this book.

But for the chakra prayer-meditation, the fact that there are three extra phrases poses a challenge. What to do with them? Over the last thirty years I've tried different solutions. I will describe three of my favorites here.

You could of course just leave these three phrases out when doing the chakra meditation. That doesn't work for me, but it might for you. In my case, my mind doesn't want to accept the prayer as complete without them. I learned the prayer with twelve phrases as a child, and what we learn as a child is deep within us.

Here are some of the ways I have worked energetically with these phrases: For Thine is the Kingdom, and the Power, and the Glory, Amen.

"Kingdom" corresponds to the 10th path, of "I build/use." Here we have the path of political leadership. But we declare to ourselves with this phrase that—no matter how strong our personal power may appear—it is always "Your Kingdom" we strive to actualize. And Your Kingdom is one of love, kindness, care, fairness, etc.

"Power" corresponds to the 11th path, of "knowledge," and the saying "Knowledge is power" comes to mind here. The phrase reminds us that no matter what advances we make in science, we align ourselves with the higher self that does not wish to impose itself on others.

"Glory" corresponds to the 12th path of "I believe." It represents the ecstatic mystic in us, the self-sacrificing part that is nourished by appreciating the glorious and the beautiful in life.

I will talk about each of these aspects in more detail in Part Two. But first, here are some of the ways I have taken these phrases into the Chakra Prayer-Meditation.

1.) Charging the Energy Bodies:

Sense the energy of the phrases in your energy bodies:

Kingdom—physical body and etheric body (an inch around the physical body.

Power—emotional and mental bodies (about 12 – 18 inches around the physical body).

Glory—in your outermost, so-called "cosmic" or "spiritual body" (extending several more feet around the physical body).

However—and this is important—at the end of the prayer, come solidly back into your physical body again. Otherwise you'll be spaced out of your body all day and even during your sleep, and, if you are anything like me, you'll be accident prone and unable to get into a truly deep sleep.

AT THE END OF THE PRAYER, regardless of how you incorporate the last three phrases, find yourself solidly grounded either deep within yourself in your heart, or in your feet.

So in this case, as you say, "Forever and ever," travel back from your cosmic energy body into your physical body and find the eternal spirit of "home" in your heart center and stay there for a moment. Feel your body solidly before you move. Tense up your muscles to feel your body more strongly if need be.

I can't stress how crucially important it is not to go on an energetic ego trip and surround oneself with light and "get high" on the sense of higher mental imagery and not find oneself solidly back in one's body before closing the prayer. To function in the world and to stay healthy physically and emotionally a complete and sound connection to the body is essential.

2.) Protecting the body, activating the heart:

Kingdom—feel your feet. You walk in the Kingdom of Spirit.

Power—Feel the top of your head. Your power is linked to the greater power of spirit that enters your body through the chakra at the top of your head.

Glory—Feel your heart chakra. Here you treasure life, you "marvel" in the "glory" and miracle of it all.

3.) Solidifying your Path and Stance:

Kingdom, Power, and Glory are all said and visualized beneath the feet. Your path of life is firmly anchored in these phrases.

AMEN

The word "Amen" is related to the word "Om" in that both contain a sense of eternity, of coming directly from Source, and of returning to Source. If you do say Amen or Om, let it be sacred to you.

Part Three

A map for the
12 Archetypal Life Paths
of Astrology

The 12 Life Paths Meditation channels the spiritual impulses inherent to the Lord's Prayer (as discussed in Part One) into the twelve divisions of the Zodiac circle, that are also the twelve archetypal paths of life.

The prayer meditation can be done in several ways. In this book, I describe a basic approach: We imagine that we are sitting or standing in the middle of the circle of the Zodiac with its twelve divisions. Each phrase of the Lord's Prayer is then spoken in its appropriate section, inviting us to contemplate the implications of that impulse for our personal life and attitudes.

On the following pages, I describe the symbolic foundation of astrology. These symbols combine to form a language of meaning. This meaning has little to do with popular astrology, but is intriguing as a representation of 12 main archetypes of life.

After this basic discussion, I will talk about the 12 Life Paths Meditation and provide a page of instructions that you can record or read to yourself until you have them memorized. I will then repeat a section from Part One that relates each phrase of the Lord's Prayer to its corresponding life path from astrology. I'll talk personally about the Lord's Prayer meditation, and about ways to "make it your own."

Basics of Astrology

Ancient astrologists conceived of twelve human types based on two symbolic structures, 1) the three metaphoric "laws" of motion, and 2) the four metaphoric elements of nature.

Beginning with the image of the wheel—considered the first great invention of civilization—they described three distinct qualities of movement:

1)   The rim of the wheel touches the earth and moves over it. You measure how much movement there has been by how much of the rim has touched the earth and how often this movement has repeated. This strong forwards movement is called "initiation" in astrology-speak. (Each moment that the rim moves over the earth, a new state is initiated.)

2)   The center of the wheel, where the axel would be, remains apparently motionless, or "fixed." It is always in the center of the wheel. This is a quality of apparent non-movement. But of course, the center moves forward along with the entire wheel. But in its apparent non-movement, it provides dynamic stability to the whole

3)   The spokes of the wheel. These run between the rim and the axle, distributing pressure and enabling the wheel to function. This quality is called, simply, "movement." But the movement is not forward, as with the rim. Here the movement is meditative—it communicates between the center and the rim.

These qualities are interpreted as basic personally types:

1)   Those of us who are the wheel's rim put projects into motion. "Let's do this new thing! It'll be great," says the rim of the wheel.

2)   The axle thinks it over. The axel does not like change, but if the idea is a good one, the axle will say, "Okay. I'll go there with you."

3)   Then the spokes/mover says, "Oh, tell me what to do, I'd love to be a part of this project!"

The first type gets things started (an impulse-type), the second either enables or disables the impulse (a will-type), and the third willingly does the footwork for getting it done (a cooperative work-type).

Astrologists then looked at the four elements:

1) The fire type is passionate, self-assured, energetic, and focused largely on him or herself, or with matters of spirit.

2) The earth type is conservative, slow moving but determined, and focused on material matters, or matters of the earth.

3) The air type is mental, concerned with communication, law, science, social and intellectual matters.

4) The water type is emotional, receptive, encompassing, nurturing, and concerned with the matters of the soul.

One set of metaphors contains three variables, and the other contains four, so the result is twelve distinct combinations:

1)	Initiative – Fire	Aries	"I am"
2)	Fixed – Earth	Taurus	"I have"
3)	Movement – Air	Gemini	"I think"
4)	Initiative – Water	Cancer	"I feel"
5)	Fixed – Fire	Leo	"I will"
6)	Movement – Earth	Virgo	"I work"
7)	Initiative – Air	Libra	"I judge"
8)	Fixed – Water	Scorpio	"I desire"
9)	Movement – Fire	Sagittarius	"I understand"
10)	Initiative – Earth	Capricorn	"I build"
11)	Fixed – Air	Aquarius	"I know"
12)	Movement – Water	Pisces	"I believe"

The twelve combinations constitute the basis of the twelve personality types and *are* key to the twelve life paths signified by the Zodiac divisions. I recommend that the interested reader research more about astrology in classical works of astrology (rather than popular works). Astrology represents a fascinating map of life and study of the human personality.

I will repeat in the next section the correspondences between the Lords Prayer, and the 12 Life paths that you also found in Part One so that you can review it here. The Life Path Meditation begins immediately after.

The Twelve Paths

1) **Aries – *I am*.** "I am that I am" — without question. I live from the simple feeling of having an unending source of energy. The restless traveler, achiever and risk taker. Initiation into novelty.

2) **Taurus – *I have*.** I take on form. I enter into and am concerned with the material side of existence. I forget that my nature is pure spirit and become very attached to beauty in form. The lover of luxury and gratification.

3) **Gemini - *I think*.** Some say, "I speak." I conceptualize, name, communicate. I connect through words and describe the world. The journalist, traveler, tradesperson.

4) **Cancer - *I feel*.** I connect through my senses with everything. Intuitively, I understand. Through deep, concentrated feeling, I open the door to my spiritual heart center. The mother, nurse, community organizer.

5) **Leo – *I will*.** I create through my will and intentions. I shine from inside out and want to be acknowledged. Artists, actors, musicians, gamblers, leaders.

Corresponding Phrases

1) *Our Mother / Father / Source* – We turn our attention and reverence toward our own Pure Being, the "I am" state of blissful consciousness of being one with everything at the 7th chakra.

2) *In Heaven* – Pure Being takes on form, is 'in heaven.' Self-identity as a spiritual being. But not in pure bliss. The beginning of ego or self orientation in dualistic based realities. The 6th chakra.

3) *Hallowed be your Name* – Pure Being is conceptualized and named. 5th chakra at the throat.

4) *Your Kingdom Come* – The energetic home of Source in the body and aura is at the heart, the 4th chakra. Ramana Maharishi gives this chakra as the focus for meditation on self.

5) *Your Will be done, on Earth as in Heaven* – Pure Being enters the emotional-energetic state of the 3rd chakra of intention and creativity.

6) *Virgo - I work.* Also, "I analyze." I bring myself fully into life, with my energy and my ability to plan, so that I can provide food and shelter for myself and my community. The accountant, biologist, or anyone who brings great attention to detail in their work. SERVICE

7) *Libra - I judge.* Also, "I balance." I live communally under common laws. I unite opposites and create harmony. The judge, the legislator, the town gossip.

8) *Scorpio - I desire.* I long for extreme experiences and I seek fulfillment. Through sexual pleasure, I regenerate myself and procreate. The Philosopher, the extremist, the occultist.

Corresponding Phrases

6) *Daily Bread* – Pure Being acknowledges the need to work to feed oneself and one's family and community, accepting inter-dependency without becoming co-dependent. 2nd chakra just above pubic area, metabolizing of intra-human experiences.

7) *Forgive us our debts, as we forgive our debtors* – here pure Being acknowledges community life and laws, ethical considerations, karmic debts and commitments. 1st chakra at the base of the spine, where, in one aspect, one's plan of life is laid out in the form of karmic debts to resolve.

8) *Lead us not into temptation* – Here Pure Being acknowledges that desire can lead to great works and wisdom, but initially, it may lead us through valleys of darkness. We ask for guidance in the school of desire, so that we can learn discrimination and continue to grow. Second aspect of 1st chakra – extreme experience: sexuality, kundalini energy, reproduction, death.

9) *Sagittarius - I understand.* Also, "I see," and "I lead." I study higher learning, I understand subtle aspects of life, I perceive far-reaching consequences. Therefore, I can lead others. The philosopher, teacher, priest.

10) *Capricorn - I build.* Another form is "I use." I construct and organize structures for society's future, such as institutions and politics that affect the world. The lawyer, the politician, the CEO.

11) *Aquarius - I know.* The individualist who seeks to expand knowledge. The inventor. The altruist—or the opposite.

12) *Pisces - I believe.* Compassionate. I am filled with awe and gratitude for the gift of life, and return deep devotion to the spirit source. The artist. The Mystic. The poet. The intuitive scientist.

Corresponding Phrases

9) *Deliver Us from Evil* – Here Pure Being focuses on deliverance from the down-pulling forces of our own earth-nature, so that we are not shortsighted, bent on desire-satisfaction, but far-sighted, able to comprehend consequences and cultivate values, and so that we can respond to wise teachings and leadership, and later, provide teaching and leadership to others.

10) *For Yours in the Kingdom* – Here we affirm that the human society we build together is ultimately one that must evolve to meet the needs of developing spiritual human beings. Our plans must project from the spiritual heart.

11) *Yours is the Power* – Here we affirm that the greatest power on earth is that of caring. When we care, when we make the welfare of everyone our own concern, we are linked into the force of Source.

12) *Yours is the Glory* – Here we affirm that reverence, or gratitude and devotion towards God, is necessary to being a complete human being. We call this here in churchy language: 'Giving God the Glory.'

The Twelve Life Paths Meditation

- Sit easily on the floor or chair. If the latter, sit with legs uncrossed, feet flat on the floor, hands on thighs, palms up, fingers gently open.

- Breathe deeply and slowly three times.

- Shake your hands gently to release any tension and place them on your thighs again.

- Ask that your mind and heart be open to the vision of the White Light. You can ask now that "Healing White Light," or "Light of Protection," or "Light of Love and Peace" or other name come to you now and enter the room where you are sitting.

- Envision the Light entering your room, rising up from the floor to the ceiling, and filling the room. It is flowing in a spiral motion; it leaves no space unfilled: it lights beneath the furniture, the tables and beds, behind all the furniture and curtains, even in the drawers and closets. The White Light fills the room and penetrates the walls, doors, and windows, filling the corners and pressing up to the ceiling. It brings us: peace, love, harmony, balance, self-control, and understanding.

- Breathe deeply and feel the energetic change in the room and around your body. Envision the light circling one inch around your body, from your feet to your head. Envision the light circling five inches around your body. Now envision the light circling ten inches around your body.

- Feel the closeness of the light, with its peace and love, and feel the release of negative emotions and physical tensions. If you would like, shake your hands gently to release any tension. Imagine that this energy turns into dust.

- If you would like to deepen the experience more, do steps 7 and 8 as described on pages 24-25.

Basic Twelve Life Paths Meditation

Imagine sitting or lying in the center of a circle. It is divided into 12 sections. You are facing (or your head is lying in the direction of) the apex of the Zodiac, or highest point in the sky, where the 10th path begins. Behind you (or if you are lying, at your feet) begins the 4th path. To your left begins the 1st, and to your right begins the 7th.

1. To your left begins the first life path, the "I am." Think about your basic feelings of self-worth, about how you see yourself as a person, and the importance you give to yourself as a person. Speak "Our Father" (Mother, Source, etc.) into this division, to remind you of your higher self, and to bring a healing impulse to your sense of self.

2. To your left but down 30 degrees begins the second life path of "I have," where one's person takes form materially in terms of one's body, house, car, garden, art collection and so on, and including one's financial capital. Speak "Who art in Heaven" into this path to remind yourself that while no material possession lasts forever, the material and financial matters of this earth should be honored, cultivated and tended.

3. Another 30 degrees onward to your left and behind you begins the third life path of "I think" that expresses itself in language and communication. Our basic thought patterns are formed when we learn structures of language from our parents. Thoughts can take on a life of their own, can speed up, race, or be compulsive. Some of us have slow thoughts, or brain damage, and we cannot find the words we seek. Speak "Hallowed be thy name" into this division to be conscious of your use of language and to remind yourself that language has an innately divine/energetic essence.

4. Directly behind you begins the forth life path of "I feel." It is appropriate that it is behind you (or below you), as our feelings are largely subconscious. This is the life path of the home, of early childhood imprinting. This is where we are emotionally rooted in self. Speak "Thy Kingdom come" into this division to bring healing to the inner child, and to acknowledge our wish that love and forgiveness rule in our lives.

5. Thirty degrees more to your right begins the fifth life path of "I will" that expresses itself in creativity and intention. In life, we can be consciously and purposefully creative or we can be impulsive and may hurt others or ourselves in the process. Speak "Thy will be done" into this division, to bring consciousness into your creative energies, and to align them with your higher self.

6. Thirty degrees farther brings you to the sixth life path of "I work" that expresses itself in acceptance and joy in the duties and tasks of everyday life. This is also the division of physical health—for how we metabolize and detoxify has a lot to do with our fundamental attitudes about what life has demanded from us, or what it requires from us that we may or not agree with. Working for the well-being of ourselves and our family is an honor that we can accept or resist. Speak into this division "Give us this day our daily bread" to help bring adjustment to your attitude about the necessities of life, to help you find clarity about what it is that you really feel called to do

and how you can best go about accomplishing that, and also to express gratitude for what you have received.

7. Directly to your right begins the seventh life path of "I balance" that expresses itself in relationships, in partnership, and in the laws that enable communities to get along. We may either accept the limitations implicit in sharing resources with other people, or we may become reclusive and not acknowledge the necessity for politeness, compromise and so on. Speak "Forgive us our debts, as we forgive our debtors" into this division to bring strength or adjustments to your attitudes and understanding, and to bring emotional release from any resentment or guilt that you may harbor relating to these issues.

8. Thirty degrees onward begins the eighth life path of "I desire" that expresses itself in the most powerful experiences of human life: being born and dying, sexual regeneration, and spiritual transformation. Here, we enter commitments and contracts, and here, too, we encounter our desire for power over others. Speak, "And lead us not into temptation" into this division to remind yourself of the higher purpose of desire: that it slowly transform into the desire to be one with oneself, true to oneself, and good to oneself and all of humankind and all of life.

9. Thirty degrees farther begins the ninth path of "I understand" that expresses itself in grasping large

perspectives and bodies of knowledge. Those who achieve great understanding might go on an ego-trip with it, or they may and use their understanding to guide others and to direct the course of human activity in a good and sustaining direction. Speak "Deliver us from evil" into this division, to remind yourself that your higher self seeks the highest truth and most positive outcome. Your higher self hopes that one day, you will be a great teacher for others, so that all of humanity can be reached and elevated.

10. Directly in front of you (or in the direction of your head if you are lying) begins the tenth path of "I build" that expresses itself in your creating and participation in culture. This is where who you are shines in the world and is where others feel your influence. On this archetypal path we might develop an ego-trip, as do many politicians, or we could keep in mind that our work is in the service of a higher purpose and that we are very small in the scheme of things. Speak "For thine is the Kingdom" to remind yourself that everything you build on earth is transient, and yet it contributes to what will come in the future; your 'influence' is best placed in the service of that "Kingdom."

11. Thirty degrees onwards to your left begins the eleventh path of "I know." Here we acquire knowledge. We are innovative. We invent new ways of doing things, new technology, and new approaches to living as human

beings. This is where we commune with our friends and where we dream of a better future, for in our dreams are the seeds of what one day may be. Knowledge is said to be power, and true knowledge must be acquired for our dreams to one day be manifested. Speak "Thine is the power" into this division, to remind yourself that the power and the future you hope for depend on your understanding the deeper nature of higher self's knowledge and power.

12. Thirty degrees onwards begins the twelfth life path of "I believe" that expresses itself in the joy, gratitude and the pure wonder we sometimes feel for the privilege to be alive and thus part of life's mystery. This wonder may be expressed through personal joy and through artistic and mystical expression such as poetry, music, art, theater, and also in the service to others. The acute sensitivity of such feelings however can lead to difficult mood swings. To dull such feeling, excessive food and alcohol, drug abuse, compulsive behavior and so on may become a pattern. Or one may go on an ego-trip with one's artistic expression. Speak "Thine is the glory, forever and ever" into this path to remind yourself of the fact that life always was and always will be infinitely marvelous, a miracle that is beyond comprehension. Let the whole compass of your life, all twelve archetypal paths, express themselves in honor of this mystery so that you can grow into it and become one with the simple and eternal joy of being.

1. On the first path, that of being, where the "I" says "I am," speak the words, "Our Father (Father-Mother, or Source)

2. On the second path, that of becoming, where the "I" says, "I have," speak the words, "Who Art in Heaven"

3. On the third path, that of conceptualization, where the "I" says, "I speak," speak the words, "Hallowed be thy Name"

4. On the forth path, that of becoming rooted in self, where the "I" says, "I feel," speak the words, "Thy Kingdom Come"

5. On the fifth path, that of will power and creativity, where the "I" says, "I will," speak the words, "Thy Will be Done"

6. On the sixth path, that of employment, where the "I" says "I work," speak the words, "Give us this day our daily bread"

7. On the seventh path, of partnerships, relationships, and of laws, and where the "I" says "I judge," speak the words, "Forgive us our Debts, as we forgive our Debtors"

8. On the eighth path, of sexuality, death and regeneration, where the "I" says, "I desire," speak the words, "And lead us not into temptation"

9. On the ninth path, of insight, knowledge, teaching, and leadership, where the "I" says, "I see," speak the words, "But deliver us from evil"

10. On the tenth path, of culture, and of high human expression on earth, where the "I" says, "I build," speak the words, "For Thine is the Kingdom"

11. On the eleventh path, that of knowledge and altruism, where the "I" says "I know," speak the words, "And Thine is the power"

12. On the twelfth path, that of mystic experience, where the "I" says, "I believe," speak the words, "And Thine is the glory, forever and ever, Amen"

Conclusion

Make this journey your own

What happens during these meditations can be very self-revealing. For instance, I sometimes get stuck when I arrive at a division where I am actually experiencing problems in my life. I begin to dream or dose off, and then have to start over again. It is as if something in me does not want to look at whatever is happening, and my mind plays tricks on me to help me avoid it.

Then I repeat the particular phrase of the Lord's Prayer that coincides with the life path I am struggling with, and I contemplate what the words mean and how that particular life path energy wants to express itself. I ask for healing for that path of life.

The same for the Lord's Prayer Chakra meditation. I will be descending through the chakras and suddenly lose track of where I am. I might repeat the prayer several times, starting at the top of the head, but always drifting off at exactly the same point. Finally, I will increase my focus, realizing that there is something going on in a particular chakra/area of life that needs special attention. When I arrive at that chakra again, I look closely at what is going on and at what I don't want to see. Sometimes I can sense here tensions building from situations in my life that do not have immediate solutions, and that therefore affect my entire energy system. I bring the impulse of the Lord's Prayer to that chakra.

Keep a Diary

If these meditations turn out to be lifetime companions for you, as they are for me, you may want to keep a diary, briefly jotting down what you experience, where you are blocked, which insights open up to you, and so on. In later phases of your life, this diary may help you appreciate your transformations over the years.

Rewrite the Lord's Prayer – Make it Personal

Rewriting this great prayer can be a great exercise, as it reflects back to you your present attitudes and understanding about the paths of your life. Putting your thoughts into words challenges you to be absolutely clear. Here is one version as an example.

Oh my Source, my Mother-Father Creator,

May your transcendental form be the light of my mind,

So that all my concepts, thoughts and words are in honor of you,

And may heart mature, so that I can resonate in your love, compassion and joy, and share it with others,

And may my will be strong and in tune with you

And my actions in daily life, and in my learning, employment and dealings with others be done in thankfulness,

And may my karmic debt run its course without causing further indebtedness

And may I forgive all who are indebted to me, past, present and future,

And may my sexuality be whole and joyful, and my inner transformation ongoing

And may all the paths of my life run to You

For Your Life-force is my Life-force

And your power is the only real power

And all that is, above and below, is in honor of you.

Amen/Om.

Another Example:

Our Source,

Transcendental,

Your Name is a Sacred Bridge to You,

Your Love reign in my Heart,

Your Will guide my Will.

May I joyfully work within the human community,

And be moderate in pleasure, finding You within it

And may I heed Your guidance and wisdom in all things, so

that all the ways of my life lead me to You.

For ultimately, only Spirit endures.

Amen / Om.

About the Author:

Dana Williams has lived in Europe and the United States. She is a stay-at-home mother of four children. Her hobbies are music and horseback riding. She says she maintains her health with diet, yoga and meditation. She believes that her personal healing visualizations have helped her overcome a debilitating disease. Dana Williams does not regard herself as a spiritual teacher, yet she would like to share the spiritual experiences that have sustained and enriched her life and health.

Other Books by Dana Williams:

Math by Grace:

Memorization of basic math for concentration-challenged children through relaxation and meditation techniques.

disorder = dɪs 'ɔːd ə

Devil = 'dev ᵊl

evil = iːv ᵊl

visualization = vɪʒ u əl aɪ 'zeɪʃᵊn

raising (my family) = выращивание (эй)

rising (up) = поднимающийся (ай)

sacred (эй) - священный

spiral (ай) - спираль

solar plexus (солнечное сплетение) = səʊ lə pleks əs

naval

abdomen (брюшная полость) = æb d əm ən

genitals = 'dʒen ɪ təl

loins (поясница) = lɔɪn z

thighs (бёдра) = θaɪz

void = (пустота)

heaven = 'hev ən

Zodiac = 'zəʊd iæk

- Aries = 'eər iːz (овен)

- Taurus = tɔːr əs (телец)

- Gemini = 'dʒem ɪ naɪ (близнецы)

loins = lɔɪn z (поясница)

groin = grɔɪn (пах)

thighs = θaɪz (бёдра)

flanks = flæŋks (бока)

hips = (бёдра)

- go around in circles
- short-sighted
- far-sighted

---

acknowledge = ək'nɒlɪdʒ
delve = (копался, рылся) delv

---

reverence = (благоговении)
throat = θrəʊt (горло)
chakra = 'tʃʌkrə
aura = ɔːrə
Glory = glɔːri

---

horor = 'ɒnə
forehead = 'fɔːhəd
impuls = 'ɪmpʌls
Hallowed = 'hæləʊd (освящённый)

---

intestines =/(кишечник) = ɪn'testɪnz
torso = 'tɔːsəʊ (торс, туловище, корпус)
abdomen = (живот) = 'æbdəmən
bond (связь) = bɒnd
bone (кость) = bəʊn
womb (матка) = wuːm
typically = 'tɪpɪkəli
harvest = 'haːvɪst

1 овен	Aries	'eər iːz
2 телц	Taurus	tɔːr əs
3 близнецы	Gemini	'dʒemɪ naɪ
4 рак	Cancer	'kænt s ə
5 лев	Leo	'liː əʊ
6 дева	Virgo	'vɜːg əʊ
7 весн	Libra	'liː brə
8 скорпион	Scorpio	'skɔːp i əʊ
9 козрог	Sagittarius	sædʒ ɪ 'teəriəs
10 стрелц	Capricorn	'kæprɪ 'kɔːn
11 водолей	Aquarius	ə 'kweər i əs
12 рибн	Pisces	'paɪs iːz

Ⴑ calves = kɑːvz (икра ноги, голенб, телёнок)
                                             телята

zodiak = 'zəʊ di æk
phrase = 'freɪz

glory = gˈlɔːri
path = pɑːθ
amen = ˈɑːmen
zodiak = ˈzɒʊ diæk

impulse = ˈɪmpʌls
compass = ˈkʌmpəs
astrology = əˈstrɪʌ tʌdʒi
image = ˈɪm ɪdʒ
civilization = sɪvəˈlɑːˈzɪʃˈn
rim = ʌʊʒɪ̩ʊpɑʊ

movement = ˈmuːv mʌnt
Lord's Prayer = ˈlɔːidz ˈpreɪə
acknowledge = əkˈnɒlɪdʒ
division = dɪˈvɪʒən

miracle = ˈmɪr ʌkʌl
Hallowed = ˈhælˈ ʌʊd
debtors = ˈdetə z